C0-ALM-512

THE MAZE

THE MAZE

Poems by Mick Fedullo

Published by The Galileo Press   Baltimore   1985

Copyright © 1985 by Mick Fedullo

Grateful acknowledgement is made to the editors of the publications in which the following poems first appeared:

Antaeus: "Strip Mining"
Chicago Review: "Trees"
Choomia: "A Toast to Thomas Eakins," "In My Brother's House"
Iowa Review: "The Shadows" (under the title, "Blue Nude")
Quarry West: "The Fish: 1964"
Sonora Review: "The Singer," "At His Mother's Grave in the Desert"
Telescope: "An Old Woman's Cottage Burns," "Ira Hayes," "Visiting Thomas at the State Hospital"
Water Table: "Travelling from Pennsylvania to Arizona"

The following poems first appeared in the chapbook, *In My Brother's House* (Porch Publications, 1979): "A Walk in the Woods," "Harry" (in a different version and under the title, "The Saint from Village Green"), "The Horse," "What to Say"

Cover art: Collage of handmade paper, by Helen Frederick
Cover design by Jack Stephens

ISBN 0-913123-06-4 (cl.)
ISBN 0-913123-04-8 (pbk.)

Library of Congress Catalog Card Number: 84-81136
All Rights Reserved

First Edition

Published by The Galileo Press, 15201 Wheeler Lane, Sparks, Maryland 21152

To Julie Willson

Contents

The Shadows
after Matisse

It is finally that we have nothing to assume
Of ourselves but shadow:
The one infallible proof
That we survive the light.

The buildings falling over
The trees and asphalt
Convince me that there are places to go,
But I will wait.

And if I waited until the hour
Just before the first light,
Still, I think you would arrive;
And we would return

Through the same streets of sketchy light
To the same room,
Dawn throwing itself at the windows;
And against the same white wall

The long, dark curves of your body
Once again
Would erase all doubt.
And here, if I wanted,

If I thought it would make you smile,
I would talk about the moon that night;
But we both know
It is the unseen side

That is fullest,
The black tree lying on the ground
That calls the birds in.
In the park, it is the shadow

Of the fountain that assures me;
The black water rushing out, then back,
Over grass that is half grass, half shadow,
And the bench where I sit,

Waiting for you,
Is rooted in its own perfect nothingness,
As a man thinking of death,
Able to live fully by it.

The Singer

1.

When she turned eleven
And the simple
Stain of life
Spread between her legs,
And her breasts rounded,
She withdrew,
Day by day, into communion
With her bedroom mirror,
Matching lyrics
To expressions, and we,
Her brothers,
Taunted her endlessly
From the yard
Below her window.

My little sister became a woman,
And under the eucalyptus
In our backyard
She married a man our father's age.

Days I'd visit
She would be singing,
Not for talent's sake,
But ambition's.
She had preposterously beautiful
Red hair,
And moved about
Graceful as a shadow on water.

Marriage could not keep her.

2.

It was not music that grew
Inside of her,

And the pressure and pain,
She was told,
Would not cease
Until the last
Flames of her life had
Burnt out. It would be soon.

The ancient,
Human surprise,
"*I* am an *I*,"
Dazzled her,
Frightened her
In her absolute vulnerability.

Soon her speech
Broke down,
Twisted like a face losing
Its musculature,
Though on occasion she sat up
In bed, propped against her pillows,
And queerly broke
Into song.

I'd watch her throat as
She tried at last
To maintain some far away
Inaudible note,
And all of us,
My brothers, my mother and father,
Aunts and uncles,
Encouraged this to no end.

At her instruction one morning,
I removed
From her bedroom the mirrors,
And all glass objects:
Vases, water glasses, picture frames,
So that she could
Avoid contact
With the poisoned,
Hairless rat

She said she had become.
And then it was all over.

I remember we were asked to turn
To such and such a page
In our hymnals,
So as to sing
For her a few, pathetic songs,
And it was over.

3.

The other night,
When we made love until dawn,
When you said
At no time had it been better,
That wonderful night, I've got to
Tell you, I
Recurrently thought of my sister.

She's so beyond compassion,
But I thought of her,
And how any circumstance
Could deceive us.
I thought of her in the leaves
That cracked and rattled
Against the jalousies.
I thought of her
In the clock barely ticking
Above us.
I thought of her in the low
Monotonous voice
Of the refrigerator,
And in the weak scent of orchid
I could almost see her
Coming toward me.

It seemed then
That wisdom was nothing
If not the joke

Being played on us
Every minute of our lives.
Even walking beneath the trees
At night
We are the shadows
Of what had always
Been probable, the conditions
Of which we had
All along been senseless to.

What can we do
But bless ourselves
And go on
Singing?

4.

I thought of my sister
And did not sleep.
Toward daybreak, as I lay
Peacefully on my back,
The sun's first
Light coming in,

I imagined her,
Calm as smoke,
Dissolving into the air
As she rose,
A stain undoing itself,
Going
In all directions at once,
Never looking down on us
In our pleasure and our sadness.

In My Brother's House
for Leonard

Until the age of five
My hair was blond.
Then it changed,
Darkened, as though
A cloud had settled
Just above my head

To stay. My brother
Understands me
At times so well
I can see myself
Running to hide
In his mouth when

He is silent. I
Remember the attic
We would go to
As children; we knew
That there the secrets
Of the house

Revealed themselves,
And there, we too
Could be understood.
Secretly, we
Would pluck one wire
On the inside

Of the dusty, ragged
Piano, and that note
Spread, circled us
As though we were
A fire, around which
The ritual of love

Was being performed.
Under the naked beams
We listened and
Listened. It was a life
Rising, a life settling.
And now, unlucky in love,

I have come to talk
With my brother, and
Before he says a word,
In the quiet as he hands
Me a glass of bourbon,
I hear that note

Again and feel at home.

Joe The Face

The usual moonlight
Stripping all color from
The flowered, linoleum floor.
Joe hunches across from me.
The bar, his bar, is closed.
At the end of this pier
Jutting into the Atlantic, we are alone,
Waiting for the rat.
Joe is staring down the twin barrels of a shotgun.
"Binoculars to eternity," he tries to joke.
On the cobalt blue table-top
A bottle of sour mash
Slowly surrenders to Joe's long, uncompromising
Thirst. "We're going to be here
For eternity," I mutter.
"It'll be back," Joe snaps,
"The stinking bastards always come back for more. . ."
I think to myself
How goddamm heartless this old man is;
All he can turn over
In his mind
Is that rat, not the smallest blessing
For anyone or anything.
Why should I have to be here, at the edge of nowhere,
Between the sand and the sharks?
Joe strikes
A wooden match to light
The oil lamp. I look up at him
And, nothing better to do,
Try to figure why
They've always called him "The Face";
A face now deeply etched
By salt air, by the crazy, possessive scratch-marks
Of booze.
All at once it rushes over me.
For the first time, with firelight fitting

Tightly over his features,
I notice that he is extraordinarily handsome.
I had never thought
Of anyone as being handsome,
But, old and drunk as he is, he is extraordinarily
Handsome. I twitch, and,
Without thinking, say, "You're sick."
"Screw you, kid."
Sea water laps against the pilings,
And I glance
Down at my own legs,
Like piers at the end of which I find myself
Always out of place.
Joe lays down another belt, and I hear
His sandpaper voice:
"It's a terrible time a man must bear
To learn to love the demons
In himself.
I can dance with myself, kid, so screw you."
Of course I didn't understand.
I felt as locked in my age
As I had imagined him to be in his.
When the rat appeared
From behind the bar,
He emptied both
Barrels.

The Fish: 1964

They have trawled for fish all day,
Bringing back mountains of flounder,
And from this distance I cannot tell
Which figure is my father, as
Orange light douses each blank face.
My toes extend forever beyond the last planks.
It is as if all of these men are my father,
Each with a gift he will place in my hand,
And I will scrape and clean for hours,
Careful as a man cutting diamonds.

The Man From Rio De Janiero

"Awakening one morning
To the day's first hunger,
And sickened for so many years
By my disfigured face,
I began the series of operations.

The mirror my guide, having deadened
Myself with injections of Novocaine,
I cut from my chest a diamond of flesh,
And sewed it to the left hollow
Of my cheek. Within days,
It hardened and discolored, finally
Detaching itself, like a flake
Of lead paint from the wall.

Thereafter, I hid myself in the shanty,
Repeating the procedure over and over.
Within four months I came
Vaguely to resemble a man.
From the gorges and valleys I had weathered
Over my trunk
Came an expression any lady
In a dark bar might consider.
The doctors who later examined me
Called it miraculous, and I was hailed
In the marketplace as a new saint.

Now, my arms swung at my sides,
A lunchpail gripped in one hand,
And, in the other, the black spacelessness
Of my clenched fist. I walked for
The first time under the smooth
Feather palms, the flaming acacias,
Among men who were going to their jobs
As I was going to mine, tense
In the revulsion of the unnoticed.

At night I made love to whores,
Wearing always a sleek new T-shirt.
In the morning I'd try to think to myself
That I was terribly like a great artist
In my thrust to move into a new way
Of seeing myself, and in having
The strength and know-how to succeed.

Then a wave of pain would push me back,
As I thought I could never know the man
I had become, that I had broken my cocoon
Only to bring alive the desire for warmth
Which proves fatally elusive to late moths
As they bat against the illumined screen.

Before, the mystery of my humanness
Lay cleverly concealed beneath
The inhuman face. The young boys I paid
To leave melons and meats outside my door
Thought me some kind of grotesque god.
I would draw back the shade
And watch them tremble as they noticed
My dark shape, and they'd quickly grab
The paper sack full of coins and run,
Unable to shake off
The sweet, lingering odor of drugs.

Having lost the one true power
I had learned deftly to use, I now keep
Another mystery hidden inside myself,
Like the fetid clumps of moss
Lining the black cylinder of an old well.
It's the fantasy of what I might become,
Becoming unrecognizable.
I am driven late at night toward dreams
Of human flesh, which in the form of young boys
Or whores, I force myself upon, ending
The affair with the gashes of a carving knife.
And I am never caught. Never caught.
Seized by this obsession, which grows

Through my veins and muscles like a thornbush,
I no longer go outdoors, neither for work
Nor food. Each day, peasant women and youngsters
Leave meals I will, under darkness, go out for.
I hear their slow chants as they bring their
Gifts: *Saint Marcus, Saint Marcus,* and I am both
Bitter and pleased. Every day is the same.
I read my books, and I defile the dirt floor
With my body. I have time to think and remember.
I remember once watching a giant bird spider
Leap four feet through the jungle air,
Striking an unwary muskrat. With a butterfly net
I trapped him, and, ever since, he waits
In his cage in the corner of my shanty.
I throw him mice and small birds.
My spider. My love."

Strip Mining

to the preacher's daughter
on her 35th birthday

What can you do with this town?
All night,
The wind made its way
In and out of a thousand branches,
Refusing to settle.

You can sleep,
But the town will be your dream:
A nest inside a cage of bones,
A broken egg inside a nest.
You can wake believing in miracles.

Even now, the buildings
Hunch up over the streets,
Vacant, discolored.
Who is that happy stranger downstairs?
What dress will you wear today?

You can roll over on the pillow
And witness one small hope,
The spittle
Where your mouth was, turning hard.
All the husbands you've had in your sleep!

Now, choirs of light, a last nothing.
Pulling back the curtains
You open the scar.
Here are the lives.
Count them.

Her Letter, Partially Composed, 1975
Rose, 1893–1977

"You ask about
Your father's clothes.
You can take them.
You can come
And take them any time.

And of course I
Remember the last
Decade.
I'm not so old!
Who doesn't *couldn't.*

And today, as you
Mention it,
I remember most
The pink body
Of my granddaughter

Struggling to move
Out into the larger
World. . . And just now
I remember also
That famous

Photograph:
The grass was
Green, and the
Women were dead,
Some of them

Still clutching
At their children,
Who were also
Dead.
We were told

This was not
Unusual.
Not unusual!. . .
When I hang
The wash out

In my back-
Yard, an orange
And black butterfly
Quivers
At the tips of

My slippers,
Trying to make them
Be still. It has
A way of knowing
What I am, but

Is so driven
By the yellows and reds
Nothing like danger
Matters. You
Could say the same

About me: when
I go back inside
I will often sit
A long while
At the window, watching

The flowered dresses
And blouses
Blowing out like sails!
I'm not sure
Just what in this

Attracts me: that
They are *my* clothes?
Or the colors themselves?
Or the reasons I've
Chosen those colors?

Or maybe, how
Should I say it, it is
The motion, the constant
Motion, the yard
Like a small boat

On its way,
And I am always there!"

What To Say

Ok, say that
I was happy,
But that I
Was indifferent
To such partial
Truths. There
Were nights
I slumped on

The sofa, staring,
Dazed as the
Fish staring
Back at me from
Their bowl.
But then,
The fish were
Never children,

In whom dread
Sends out its
Echo. Death for
Them is merely
The surprise of
Finding, for once,
A lid closing
Over each eye.

Say that one day
There was a man
Who got up from
His sofa to walk
Through a garden
In the full out-
Rageousness of
Summer, and that

Suddenly he let
Happiness go by
Like a cloud
Over his intention
To seize it. Say
There were times,
No doubt, he could
Sober up, unlike

The fish, from his
Embalmed trance
For love, though
Most often he
Was like the young
Primitive girl, who,
Catching sight of
A whirlwind and fear-

Ing impregnation
By the seeds of
Her swirling
Ancestors,
Runs to hide in
The arms of her
Husband. Say he came
To know, through

The years, that he
Could never be-
Come less foolish
Than this, yet
Also that he
Was not, like the
Fish, an ornament
Of thoughtlessness,

A fluid nothing.
Say there were
Entire moments that
Seemed to surround
Him like a small

Garden, a garden
Whose soil he longed
To saturate with

Himself, in order to
Sustain it, as though
He were both light
And moisture; and that
He found an hour's
Amusement in
Such paradoxes
of desire. Say that

In the end, before
The mute, gaping
Witnesses, he let go,
Not to join the
Dead, but simply
To die, his future
Beyond knowing, his
Present beyond belief.

The Horse

In a field of thick fog
I come across
An ivory horse, grazing the cold grasses,
Grazing within the composition
Of his need.
I cannot see his face,
And I am bridled, as he is,
To a beautiful solitude.
In another life
I might have ridden him off to war,
Or guided him over
A tract of mud, before planting.
He lifts his great head,
And I watch him awhile in his delusion
That he is unobserved. . .
                        Lovely cloud,
Muscular tyrant of such an insignificant
Square of earth,
We are both, in our ways, constant
To the illogic of being settled
In the world. And who would have it differently?

A Toast To Thomas Eakins

Eakins, what could your scandalous
Photos have mattered

To this girl
Sitting with her bag lunch in Logan Circle?

Minutes ago I noticed her easing
Her finger down

One of your portraits in the Philly museum.
I'm almost red to admit it,

But I cannot recall
Which one, I was so taken by

Her extraordinary dedication. It seemed
She hovered like a monarch

In a wisteria
As she entered the room full of your work.

She drifted delicately, greedily
From canvas to canvas,

And I knew she had fallen in love, perhaps
For the first time.

It might occur to you, if you were me,
That she is the center of all beauty

And grace,
Around which you are orbiting

Because now, imagine!, here she is
By the drained-out fountain in Logan Circle!

And I drink
To you, Eakins, to what

You've given us, to all
The magics we are drawn to like crazed insects.

A Walk In The Woods
for K.

A figure eight
On the ice
Is the me, the you

Of it. The skater,
The flow
Of our silences,

Has been around
That path
Dozens of times.

Goddamnit, I'd like to
Create a bird
Made of ice, and

Perch him in
An ice-
Covered pine tree,

And cause him to make
Through the icy air,
A small, significant

Sound. And I want you.

*

Of course we become
Selfish
Deciding to give:

Love can be such
A privacy
Of fear and re-

25

Joicing, it makes
Me think of
Certain Indian

Ceremonies, in which
The singers plug
Both ears, converting

Sound to inner
Vibration.
Sometimes, they will

Play small, musical
Instruments
Inside their closed

Mouths.

*

Wouldn't it be funny
If, in these cold
Woods, we came across

A bird in a tree-top
Calling
Carpe diem, carpe diem?

Large men have moved
Onto the pond,
They're boring holes

Through the ice, to let
The entranced fish
Be enlightened. Like

When they took you
Out of your
Mother after ten months,

26

You comment, ever
On the quick. . .
A reluctance you wear

Like a charm.

*

Listen, love is like
A bird the size
Of an almond, flying

Into the snow.
In memory,
It is an assurance

Against the point
At which
The bird vanishes.

Remember the artist
Robert Matta?
Once he positioned

A painting on the six
Interior
Sides of a box,

Which he then sealed.
Make no mistake.
That, too, is like love,

When love goes unspoken.

Love Failing

We build arguments,

— The bamboo planes
Of distant islanders
Resting on muddy runways
In a blue jungle —

I from gin-comfort,
From the maternal embrace
Of an overstuffed chair,

Resisting the kindness
Of your assault,

You pacing just behind
A potted coleus
Which spills fountain-like
Over a little table's
Watery glass surface,

Pacing back and forth
In front of a window
Which catches
A blue sting of sky.

I notice, behind you, the long
Feather of a vapor trail —

We wait on the promise of cargo.

Travelling From Pennsylvania To Arizona

A man glides his finger from
His left shoulder
Diagonally

Down to his right ribcage
To show his scar.
This is how I've come to be here.

For days now
I have made love in the dark
To the dark. And you?

I'm thinking of those daily
Complacencies
As though pain and hatred had not

Accompanied them
Like wings. In Nebraska,
I saw raised up over the prairie

A great kite, white
As a handkerchief. Goodbye
To your sweet face, it waved,

Goodbye to your body and your
Casual gestures and
Your wonderful paintings of sunsets.

Goodbye to your temper and your fingers.
Goodbye, goodbye, goodbye!
It is written that I'm certain

To love again someday.
It is written here
By my own

Hand.

Trees
for W. C. W.

If leaves are
a complement
to the way
one sees rain

then
the complement
to how one
thinks about

the rain
which is seen
begins with
how many trees

have entered
through mists
and under what
circumstances —

innumerable
yet he knows
the feeling
he makes the poem

*

Left a little
to his own
he will begin
by saying

this mimosa
in its skirt
of latticed shade
is his mother

before and after
the history
of her illness —
the poplars

begin to seem
elegiac —
the landscape
repeats this

over and over
she was beautiful
even surrounded
by flowers

*

The desire to see
the sluggish
mimosa
as for the first

time
without name
without being re-
minded of *treeness*

is not a longing
for the child's
stupidity
though that's when

one tree stood
not for *all trees*
but for *every*
tree —

year by year
word by word
we've begun to
recognize such

31

grandeur – it's lost
in our talk of
discovery, though not
entirely to our eyes

*

You said
"the perfect type
of the man of action
is the suicide" –

too many
have believed this
for its first
and obvious sense

taking
the term "action"
to mean the act
of giving up

rather than
simply giving in
I think at least
later on

in your own life
you would have
agreed with this
and that "suicide"

might refer merely
to an excited will-
ingness to participate
in the vigil

of one's own dying –
children will
always ask
why the trees put on

their flashiest clothes
just before winter
and we will always
tell them

because of the cold
because of the cold
and when else
would it seem right?

At His Mother's Grave In The Desert

Three years
And you are still down there
Scheming no doubt
With the darkness you've had to befriend.
I know nothing of it, nor want to,
Though at times I feel
I would like to claw down under the earth
And lay next to you forever.
From the southeast
A tremendous thunderstorm is approaching,
Pushing out ahead of it
A gray-brown wall of dust, and the desert
In the monsoon winds
Again is shifting its sameness.
If I stand here long enough
I will be caught in the churning dust,
Buried, though only for minutes,
Then washed clean
By rain.
If I stand here long enough
I will be emptied of thought and feeling,
And the steady song you have sung for three years
Will seep into and crystallize
Every cell of my body.
If I stand here long enough
I will become the sculpted memorial
You demanded of me for yourself.
I remember how at the last you said —
No, sang — in a gravelly voice,
"Piss on it! Our lives are nothing more
Than sitting in an idling car,
Waiting for the passing of a long train.
Each train-car is a season.
We don't count them,
And after the train passes
We don't cross
The tracks."
Three years and the same steady song

Continues rising out of the earth
Under which you lie.
Today I bring you a simple gift:
The opened, dried fruit
Of a saguaro cactus.
Oblong and dark red in color,
It reminds me of what your tongue must be.
It sings the same song.
Here, sing together.
How I hated you. And how that hatred
Confused itself with inexplicable love,
The way the hot blowing dust
Finally intermingles with the cooling rain behind it.
One storm after another.

Florinda
San Luis, Mexico

I rub, gently,
Both the inside and outside
Of a gray,
Porcelain goblet, blue sparrows
Glazed in flight.

"Why can't we talk?"
My husband moans again to me.

And I spit into the air,
"This goblet is my head,
I'm keeping it
Clean, and empty of my husband!"

This afternoon, as any other,
The date palms cast
On the screen of the kitchen window
A shadowy grid-work
Through which my cold stare
Momentarily
Fixes on the weather-beaten hen house.
"Is he there,

Under the chickens, under their eggs?"
I whisper to myself,
Like a snake,
Then go back to washing my dishes.

My husband
Sits down at the plywood table, says,
Because every month or two
It is the same with him,
"Why can't you forget it, woman?
The bastard was no good.
What do you want, to make love to his corpse?"

I yell out to the space around me,
"I should dig up the earth floor
Under the chickens!
Is he there?"

"Bitch," he mutters.

What are my days now?
I cook for him,
I walk behind him when he goes to town,
I sleep with him,
But since that night
So long ago
When he raged, tearing our home apart,
Storming out to fulfill
His sense of duty,
I have not once addressed him,
Nor will I. . .

My eyes shift
To the gravel road
By our house
Which cuts through a stand of creosote bush
Joining, at last,
The highway to San Luis,

And I remember
When my husband and I
Were first married,
How I watched, one day, from the porch,
As a clear vision
Of Jesus Christ
Turned his back on me.
Though I longed
To hear him say my name, to beckon me,
I witnessed only
His back and his stony silence
As he grew
Smaller and smaller, going
Down that road. . .

To my death
I will allow
No man to touch me but my husband,
Though I despise him,
Though it hurts me even to feel
His breath.
Like the blue painted sparrows
On the goblets I purchased in town,
I too am caught fast
In the act of flying away
While forever
Looking back.

My poor, stupid husband,
Sitting there
With his hateful eyes
Like tiny, obsidian pebbles,
He has become the punishment
I must suffer
For my indiscretion.

I've become his.

Primitive Arts At The Museum

1. *Eskimo Mask*

Right off
I came across
A mask

Of tree bark
And fox fur,
Based on a song

Its maker had
Heard
In a dream.

Think of it!
To carve a song,
To offer form

To that which
Held its own form
Intangibly

— Tree bark and
Fox fur! —
All for the love

Of such natural,
Delightful
Inaccuracies.

2. *Red Pot*

On its shelf
This pot
Covered with

Black figures
Of lizards
Would surely

Put off the
Indian who
Sat on the high

Desert, tossing
Over her shoulder
A shimmering

Black braid,
While continuing
To fashion

Into existence
From Maricopa clay
An emptiness

She knew
Would give the pot
Many good uses.

3. *Petroglyphs*

I have seen
Better
In remote desert

Canyons, though
These will do:
A spiral of sun

Or of some datura
Induced vision;
A deer, stiff-legged,

Suspended above
A crude stream;
A tortoise; a man

– A man no doubt,
The genitals
Being etched – Perhaps

These Hohokam wished
Some part of them
Evident

Which is not and
Never will be, some
Integrity or decadence.

4. *Blue Spruce*

You will not
Find here
An enormous

Blue spruce
From the mountains
Of Montana

Upon which
Has been hung
The dried

Umbilicus
– Wrapped tightly
In turtle-skin –

Of a Cheyenne girl's
Firstborn,
Though often

He has climbed
Into the shadowy hills
– A kind of museum –

To gaze, for strength,
At this portrait
Of himself.

41

Visiting Thomas At The State Hospital

So I would like to be casual and tell him
That I am doing fine, living now in Arizona,
And that even walking a straight line
I find the desert the impossible maze
We had long ago imagined in our talk of travel.

I would like to become excited,
Describing how I have actually let a tarantula
Walk across my hand
And felt a strange kinship that I'm sure
Would sound silly or absurd or morbid.
I'd like to share with him the details
Of a day last year when,
In the laughable shade of a mesquite tree
Near the dried up bed
Of the Gila River,
Another friend, an Indian boy, and I
Discovered a dead man:
How I had never before been as startled
Into such an awareness of the sound
Of my own self and its meaningless, self-appointed
Preoccupations.

So I don't even know where to begin,
And Thomas is already telling me,
Straight as rifle-fire,
That he is god of all possible universes,
And, finding myself in the grace of such power,
I should go down
On my knees and take his hand and kiss his fingers.

2.

Thomas goes on and on like this for days,
I was told but

42

Could hardly believe of someone
Formerly so clear in his perceptions.
In graciousness, he says,
And pity, he's come to lead us
From our sins and degradation
To everlasting bliss.
What if being blissful's not what I desire,
I ask. Then you're stupid, he says.
I think when I was younger
I would have admired his simple conviction,
Would have longed to be like that,
Aloft in a chair, waving my hand in blessing
And in judgement.
When I look at his eyes I see he is right:
They are flat, unblinking and without moisture.

Where are the bright days of our cruising
Through West Chester,
Looking for trouble with bottles of vodka
Shoved under the seat?
The days such drunkenness
Subdued our nervous sexuality,
And the serious world was an object of scorn?
The days we sweated together,
Hauling crates of mushrooms, so secretive,
Out of their dark sanctuaries
And into the backs of refrigerated trucks?
Where is the unimaginably
Graceful motion of his slender fingers,
Working those astounding shapes out of clay:
The women and the birds, the horses?

I think there must be a secret, back room somewhere,
In which logic has fallen
Onto its bed, exhausted and resigned.
So what can I offer but an uneasy sadness
That's growing in equal proportion to hope's fading?
He would take my head in his hands,
As, previously, he had taken clay, and shape me
Into the landscape of his delusions.
I wonder,
What could he be seeing, seeing me now

After so many years?
What is he looking at? What part of me?

3.

And I am supreme clumsiness,
Opening the small packages I have brought him:
Candy, a few books, and some after-shave.
I am a fire burning
In a clearing in the woods, desperate
To be caught and taken away by the wind,
To be scattered about the sky
As any of the other cold points of light.
And I am unraveled by friendship's commitment,
Which I cannot keep.

I reach into my pocket, and, at his urging,
Give him what matches I have.
Through the day-room's steel-screened windows,
I see it has begun to snow,
And the trees will soon carry such burden
As is required in winter.
Someone has switched off the T.V.
In the nurses' station, a male attendant
Is caressing with his lips the mouthpiece of a telephone,
His connection with what keeps him sane.

I must catch a plane back West, I say,
                              meaning
It is painful to accept
That I cannot be responsible in any way.
Take care of yourself, I tell him,
                              meaning
I cannot help, I am powerless and ashamed.
I'll drop you a line, I assure him,
                              meaning
I will, in solitude, weep for the inevitability
Of his future,

The details of which I will never know.
And then I am silent,
                    meaning
I'm sorry, I'm sorry,
And turn and go.

Ira Hayes

*Ira Hayes, a Pima Indian, was one of
the soldiers to lift the flag at Iwo
Jima. He died, an alcoholic, at the
age of thirty-one.*

"The truth,
I'm tired of people and love returning
To that private room
Constructed for me by gin.
In it, I know where everything is.

I'm tired of people.
It seems they're always praising
What they can't avoid:
Springtime, for instance,
Its moistures, its array of usual wonders,
The tiresome poppies
Spreading down the slopes of Picacho Peak.

I love the thick windows of drunkenness,
No one can break in,
And it is difficult for me
To resent what goes on outside.
If only we could be attacked once more
By the Apaches. . . .

Over there, I was told
That the Japanese were simpleminded,
That when a tree became barren in the orchard
Two men would go out,
One would climb the tree and one
Would raise an axe.
The first man shouted, "Don't take its life!
It's promised to bear fruit this year,
It has!" They would repeat this,
And then return home laughing,
Having frightened the cherry tree
Fertile by their cleverness.

But it was me,
Me who from fear of death blossomed
Into a soldier.
I remember thinking how the eyes
Of dead Japanese
Were just like black, withering cherries.
And I didn't care, I could step right over them.

In our ancient legends,
I'itoi, Elder Brother, made a house
For himself in the shape of a round maze,
Into which he could escape
From his ungrateful people.
Give me what I need
And I'll be happy.
I am tired of people

Who look at me as though I were still
There on Iwo Jima,
Pushing up that flag
And scared out of my mind.
There is so much water between
Here and there, more than I had ever seen,
More still than can ever blow, as rain or clouds,
Across this desert."

An Old Woman's Cottage Burns

Sussex, England

"I was risen
From my sleep,
Like that frozen
Mammoth
That had been

Caught so long
Under the peninsula
Of Taimyr, by
An intense heat.
Startled into

A world I had
Forgotten, confused
By the glare and
The unconnectedness
Of simple things,

I staggered
Heavily through
An open, back door.
And the neighbors
Greeted my ghost

With the astonishment
One reserves
For the first lilies
Of springtime.
"What will you do?,"

They asked, "Was
Anything saved?". . . .
For years I had
Stuffed my shorn hair
And nail parings

In the thatch roof
Of my cottage
So that, down
To the last, they
Would be accounted

For at Judgement.
And now the stink
Of that burning hair
Rolls out of this
Early, frightening

Sun, and I am
Neither wholly left
On earth, nor
Received in Heaven.
My neighbors turn

To me saying, "Why?
Why should this
Happen?," and I know,
Without saying,
It must have been

Caused by something
Simple; perhaps
A starling got hold of
A clipping of my hair
And worked it

Through the intricate
Web of its
Filthy nest, high
In a willow tree.
From this day

Forward, I must walk
Into those moth wings
Of flame, I must become
All over again
Absolutely myself. . . .

It's funny how
The glowing sphere
Strikes me as being
As lovely and cunning
As a cat's eye,

And the young men
Are so gentle, taking
My shoulders under
A woolen wrap,
Lifting a thermos

Of tea to my lips.
I do not think,
Though,
That young men have
Souls, bless them,

But are more like
The English moths
That blackened over
The decades, until
They came to match,

Color for color,
The soot-covered
Tree trunks they
Settle and rest on,
Lightly. They

Console me, they
Are trained in
Soft, meaningless words,
But I would tell them,
If I could, that

Grief in the end
Is blank and without
Emotion, as
What finally
Must be felt,

So far away,
In the heart of
A mammoth, thawing
Under the glacial
Sun of Taimyr."

Harry

1

It's almost funny,
The way he empties a can of insect spray
On a single, helpless ant.
The way he walks into the French doors,
Like a bird who sees there
Only the sky and the coppery fields.
Or when he confides that
You're his favorite nephew, then calls you
By your brother's name.

Uncle Harry could not escape the crudest pranks
We could think of:
Short-sheets, matches wedged in his heels,
BB gun assaults. And he lived
Through these moments of terror
As the simplest of animals do, without memory.

So when my mother packed us off
To supervise his final weeks,
My brother and I could hardly have been happier.
Harry had lived his life in this house,
And used to tell us that as a child
He and his friends would sneak off
To the crest of a hill
Overlooking the farm, and get drunk.
The thrashing he would later return to
Was almost painless.
My brother and I huddled in this same place
To formulate new strategies of mischief.

But we, also, were frightened.
At night I could hear his groaning,
And I thought his head must now
Be like one of those magnificent rattles

52

I had read the Haida Indians carve for themselves.
Bearing the likeness of their owners'
Conceptions of the ultimate,
Or of love, or some other privacy,
They are brought out rarely,
And then
Kept rattling all the while
To conceal the image of such knowledge in a blur.

2.

Day by day he stiffened,
Like a cornstalk, against the chilling air.
He'd leave untouched a tray of tea and crackers.
He shrieked at the slightest parting
Of the red, opaque draperies.
It seemed now
That thoughts for him were like uncut gemstones,
Each keeping a symmetrical shape
Locked inside,
Each shape unrelated to the other.

True enough, there were moments
Of hard lucidity.
Once he looked me in the eye and muttered,
"Every man must believe he retains
Some power to enforce justice or evil.
Against the grain, I've
Been given evil,"
And he'd slip away, turning to the wall.

One day he sharply announced that he had become
Christ's brother.
Later, he crept out of the house,
And staggered up the high, grassy hill
Bordering the pasture.
Throwing up his arms, he called for his Father
To lift him into the clouds.
He had set his wallet and his keys
Neatly on the ground,

And had stripped to the silver cross
Around his neck. It was nearly dark,

Yet the light from
Chips of broken bottles
In the grass
Flashed in his eyes, like a silent congregation.
Below, the trees were crimson,
And the fields silent.
And the clouds did open,
They opened wide,
Perfectly,
In perfect forms.

Photo by Joey Perez

Mick Fedullo was born in Pennsylvania in 1949. From 1979 through 1984 he lived and worked as writer-in-residence on the Gila River Indian Reservation, Arizona. Recently, he has been teaching creative writing to students on the Crow, Rocky Boy, and Blackfeet reservations in Montana, and on the San Carlos Apache and Navajo reservations in Arizona.